Camer

The Haunted Heart of Africa

Janvier Tchouteu

TISI BOOKS

NEW YORK, RALEIGH, LONDON, AMSTERDAM

PUBLISHED BY TISI BOOKS
www.tisibooks.com

ISBN-13: 978-1-5205-5755-7

ISBN-10: 1-5205-5755-8

PUBLISHED BY TISI BOOKS

www.tisibooks.com

NEW YORK, RALEIGH, LONDON, AMSTERDAM

Printed in The United States of America

Titles by Janvier Chouteu-Chando

The Usurper: and Other Stories
Triple Agent, Double Cross
Disciples of Fortune
The Union Moujik
Splendid Comets
Flash of the Sun
Fortune Calls
Fortune's Master
Fortune's Children
The Norilsk Bears
To Be In Love and To Be Wise
The Fire and Ice Legend
The Sweetest Madness
The Grandmothers
The Hunger Fire
The Shades of Fire
Father and Sons
The Doctors
Dark Shades
Fateful Ties
The Verdict of Hades
His Majesty's Trial
Ngoko's Folly
The Usurper
The Dowry
I am Hated
The Oaf

Non-Fiction Titles by Janvier Chouteu-Chando

FALLEN HEROES: African Leaders Whose Assassinations…
BROKEN ENGAGEMENT: Why a Donald Trump Win…
THEIR LAST STAND: Donald Trump's Upset Victory…
Ukraine: The Tug-of-war between Russia and the West
THE CANARY IN A COAL MINE EFFECT:...
Cameroon: The Haunted Heart of Africa

Upcoming titles by Janvier Chouteu-Chando

The White Hawk
The Drift Home
Mortal Friends
Norilsk Bears

Quotes

You see these dictators on their pedestals, surrounded by the bayonets of their soldiers and the truncheons of their police ... yet in their hearts, there is unspoken fear. They are afraid of words and thoughts: words spoken abroad, thoughts stirring at home --- all the more powerful because forbidden --- terrify them. A little mouse of thought appears in the room, and even the mightiest potentates are thrown into panic.

Winston Churchill

"If we fight to the death against an arbitrary integration of our country into the French colonial empire, it is because we want to remain the conquering defenders of the right of peoples to self-determination. We are thus, in the service of Kamerun and Africa...we are the true craftsmen of international detente. As revolutionary nationalists, we are fighting to realize for the Kamerun and for it alone, a true national "Independence" with "Unification" as a precondition, simultaneous or consecutive, but never excluded."

Ruben Um Nyobè

"Without Africa, France will have no history in the 21st century."
François Mitterrand, 1957

"We are not involved in this struggle only because we think that we will dismantle this system in the course of our lives. We hope Cameroon changes tomorrow. But if it doesn't, we will be happy to know that we made the ground fertile for the next generation that will end the rot in this country, and then establish the "NEW CAMEROON"."
Dr. Samuel F. Tchwenko, former UPCist and chief ideologue of the historic SDF of 1990-2002

"Until the lions have their own historians, the history of the hunt will always glorify the hunter."
Chinua Achebe

"Cameroon is not a country of slaves that no man can free."
Janvier Chouteu-Chando

"To be sure, dictators are crafty, evil geniuses with awesome firepower at their disposal. They are also brutally efficient at intimidation, terrorism, and mass slaughter. However, a force is able to dominate because the counterforce is either nonexistent or weak.
George B.N Ayittey

"Africa is my country and Cameroon, my family."
Didier Banlock

"...The world gets blessed every now and then with unique souls who though burdened by their invisible crosses, still have the extraordinary strength to forge ahead in life and give others a helping hand at the same time. Despite their tribulations, most of us think they are fine. Even when the weight of their crosses become unbearable, even when they proceed in a breathless manner, we still have a hard time understanding that they are drowning. In fact, we even condemn them for failing to sacrifice more..."

Janvier Chouteu-Chando, Disciples of Fortune

"The use of political assassination against liberation movements has changed the course of history in a number of countries in Africa and continues to devastate the Middle East. The current power relations between the Third World and the dominant Western and imperialist powers, are a product of the war of attrition which the West has waged, particularly by political assassinations, which have robbed Africa and the Middle East of some of their great leaders, and weakened their important political organizations."

— Victoria Brittain

Contents

EPIGRAPH

"The time for revolutionaries with total freedom to maneuver is over."

CHRISTOPHER KWAYEP-CHANDO

DEDICATION

This book is dedicated to the loving memory of Solomon TandengMunaYakana; and to Cameroon's historic civic-nationalists and union-nationalists who dedicated their lives to the land they love or loved, and suffered deprivations and even death for the cause to alleviate the wellbeing of the Cameroonian people.

ACKNOWLEDGMENTS

My deepest, warmest and everlasting thanks to Dr. Samuel F. Tchwenko and Christopher N. Chando for their contributions in chiseling the national idea for the "New Cameroon".

Maps

African Democracy Ratings

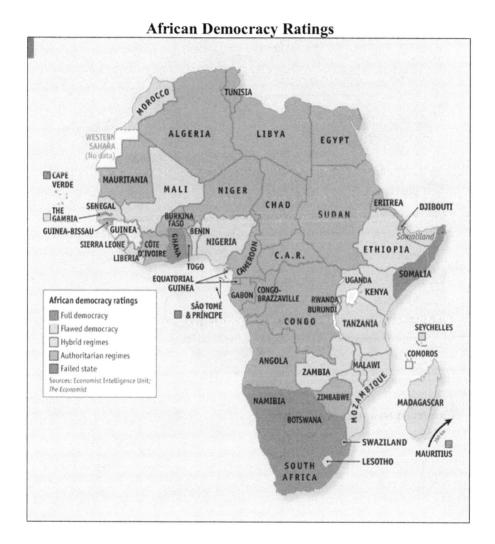

Partition Map of Africa: 1884-1914

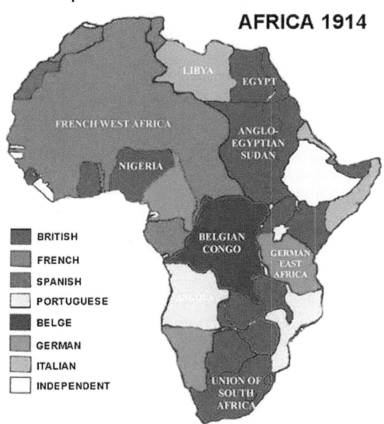

Cameroon on a map of the world

Cameroon over time

1. **German Kamerun I (1884-1911)**
2. **German Kamerun II (1911-1916)**
3. **British Cameroons&French Cameroun: 1916-1960**
4. **British Cameroons&LaRepublique du Cameroun (1960-1961)**
5. **British Southern Cameroons&La Republique du Cameroun (1960-1961)**
6. **Reunited/Independent Cameroon today.**

Introduction

Cameroon's unfinished liberation struggle is into its fourth phase already, having suffered defeat in the hands of its former colonial masters led by France, and the puppets France put in power before granting French Cameroun independence on January 01, 1960.

The Cameroonian patriots languished in defeat, but they never gave up the struggle. Today, a new generation of Cameroonian patriots variously described as the Kamerunists, union-nationalists and Cameroonian civic-nationalists picked up the baton dropped by the leaders of the country's historic UPC (Union of the Populations of the Cameroons) of 1948-1971, and the later generation civic-nationalists who joined the SDF (Social Democratic Front) in 1990-1991 believing that its leadership was committed to the struggle to complete the liberation of Cameroon. The advocates of change in these post-independence generations, who are not compromised by the anachronistic French-imposed system, oppose not only the 34-year regime of Cameroon's current head of state Paul Biya, but also the foundations of the system that Gaullist France put in place before handing power to Paul Biya's predecessor Ahmadou Ahidjo.

In these accounts, we are presented with a struggle that is not blinded by emotions, a struggle that is grounded on humanitarianism and social solidarity, a struggle that holds no rancor against the French people but rejects that fringe in the French political establishment, a political mafia per se, that is controlling Francophone Africa (FrancAfrique) and that sustains the Cameroonian dictatorship against the choice and wishes of the Cameroonian people.

PART ONE

Cameroon,
The Usurper Biya Regime
&
The Anachronistic French-Imposed System

CHAPTER ONE

The African Pearl

If you board a plane or ship plying any of the international routes and ask to be taken to the heart of Africa, do not be surprised to find yourself disembarking in Cameroon. It is a beautiful country per se, situated opposite the middle portion of Brazil, on the eastern side of the Atlantic Ocean. Bordered by six countries of which Nigeria is the most prominent neighbor, Camcroon appears on maps like a heavily pregnant mother carrying a baby on her back.

This peculiar geopolitical entity was created by accident and apportioned to Germany during the 1884 Berlin conference that carved up Africa. Thereafter, Berlin treated German Kamerun as its treasured colony for thirty-two years until Great Britain and France captured the land during the First World War, partitioned it into British Cameroons and French Cameroun, and then went on to lord it over the people for four decades. However, they too were challenged by Cameroonian civic nationalists who campaigned for the divided territory's reunification and self-rule. Today, English and French are the country's official languages, mirroring the dominance of the two Indo-European languages in Africa.

They say the gods have a design even in the most outrageous

acts of mortals. If that is the case, then it also applies to Cameroon. The country has defied so many odds in its history that the people now pride themselves on the saying that "Impossible isn't a Cameroonian word."

Renowned voices tend to call Cameroon "Africa in miniature", not only because of its fanciful shape and turbulent history, but also because of the physical and human aspects of its geography. It is the point in Africa where the East meets the West and where the North meets the South. It is a country that features plains and mountains, plateaus and valleys, rivers and seas, lakes, and waterfalls and other landmarks that mirror the rest of Africa. The south is dominated by equatorial and tropical rainforests, the north is covered by Sahelian vegetation, and the middle portion of the country is graced with high savannah of mixed grassland and forest. In fact, all the different flora and fauna in Africa can be found in this carelessly drawn triangle called Cameroon.

The curious eye is apt to notice varying statures, facial types and shades of complexion as it travels throughout Cameroon—the result of the territory's history as the crossroads of African migrations. Anthropological linguists hold that all of Africa's four major language groups converge in Cameroon.

The southern portion of the country is the base from where Bantu speakers spread to southern and eastern Africa. The furthest spread of Afro-Asiatic peoples is in the north of this territory, featuring groups like the Semitic-speaking Arabs, Berber-speaking Tuaregs, Chadic-speaking Hausas and Batas, and Fula or Fulfulde-speaking Fulanis or Peuls. Nilo-Saharan speakers dominate the north of the country in their furthest spread to the west of the African continent. Also present in Cameroon are small ethnicities of the fourth major subgroup called Niger-Congo-A that occupy the southwestern border regions with Nigeria. Settled in the northwestern portion of the country that looks like the pregnant part of Mother Cameroon is the fifth and unique indigenous group that you will find only in Cameroon. Named semi-Bantu, Graffi or southern Bantoid, this group has characteristics of all the four major language groups or sub-races in Africa. Legends and lore hold that semi-Bantus are original of Afro-Asiatic and Nilo-Saharan descent and that they assimilated all the peoples they encountered in the course of their migration. The Bamileké people are the dominant ethnicity in this group.

It is true that Cameroon's human and physical wealth has been the source of its turbulent history, its pride and the ingredients that give its people a unique flavor. The flavor has produced colorful Cameroonian characters that the curious eye and mind is likely to enjoy by hating or loving them, pitying or angrily denouncing them. These characters provide insights into human nature and the African continent that is haunted by leaders with the evil disposition.

While other African peoples have picked up arms and warred among themselves to have their country split up, Cameroon is the only geopolitical entity in the continent whose inhabitants went to war to reunite its people separated by the legacy of the Anglo-French partition of the former German colony of Kamerun. It is the only country where those who fought for its reunification and independence are yet to assume political power, as they continue to languish from the defeat suffered in the hands of the French overlords and the puppets the French political establishment installed in power in Cameroon. It is the land where you will find Africa's biggest political deception and sleaziest mafia. It is the country in Africa with the lowest number of heads of state in its history, yet it is a country that is unlikely to engage in internecine war to get rid of the suffocating system.

(Culled from Triple Agent, Double Cross)

Part II: Afterthought on 07/04/2015: Cameroon as a Hijacked Nation

In power since 1982 is Africa's absentee dictator Paul Biya, who was made the successor of his predecessor Ahmadou Ahidjo by an order from former French President Francoise Mitterrand; Ahidjo, who himself was brought to power by the French to usurp the aspirations of Cameroonians in their liberation struggle led by the UPC that the French banned in 1955, a party with more than 80% of the land's intellectuals and even more national support. France had made sure Ahidjo's power was secured by decimating its support base in a 12-year war against the party and by killing all the UPC leaders (Ruben Um Nyobè 1958, Felix Moumié in Geneva 1960, Osende Afana 1966, Ernest Ouandié 1971 etc.), leaving Cameroon a nation haunted by an "Unfinished Liberation Struggle". Today, Cameroonians are out not only to get rid of the Dictator Biya's autocracy but are also determined to do away with the French-imposed system that its custodians want to maintain with someone else at its head in Cameroon after Paul Biya departs to the world beyond.

Part III: Cameroon under an oppressive system and haunted by Terrorism.

Compounded by the retrogressive system and the lunacy of the Biya regime is the specter of Boko Haram that started haunting northern Cameroon a few years ago, a distorted form of Islam espoused by a group that sees glory in the murder of the innocent (women, children and other civilians), a spillover from Nigeria's religious tension and an amalgamation of geopolitics as foreign interests extend the exploitation of resources in the Lake Chad

Basin.

And as if to denigrate the glorious Cameroonian soul even further, the usurper regime of Paul Biya failed to address the grievances of the peoples of the English-speaking part of the country (the former West Cameroon in the Cameroon Federation of 1961-1972, and what was the former British Southern Cameroons of 1916-1961 following the partition of the former German Kamerun into British Cameroons and French), making the ground fertile for the fringe group called Ambazonia to hijack the Anglophone Cameroonian cause for democracy and federalism, by pursuing the route of secession that led to an armed struggle in late 2017. This new and ongoing conflict gives a false notion of the century-old Cameroonian struggle for the "New Cameroon" as it gives some sense of relevance to these sides that have never had the interest of Cameroon at heart --- one, falsely as the force trying to keep Cameroon together, while the other, sadly as the force to take Anglophone Cameroon away to a future that in reality is Impossible.

How then does Cameroon emerge from this surrealism where the forces engaged in an armed conflict see their only legitimacy coming from the inhuman actions of one another, and where they are basically coercing the majority of the population into tolerating their anti-people actions that go against the noble ideal of a "New Cameroon" and a "New Africa" that foreign interests have been bent on thwarting for over a century now, foreign forces that see them as nothing but "Useful Idiots" in their game plan?

Only a Cameroon rid of the retrogressive French-imposed system and headed by those who put the interest of the land above their personal interests or the interests of foreign entities who have no genuine concern for the land, can the citizens of Cameroon be certain that the country and government would be able to handle the insecurity posed by anti-people and dehumanized groups. In fact, the system/Biya regime and Boko-Haram, as well as the secessionist/separatists, are in symbiosis as they make each other relevant in a space where the vast majority of the Cameroonian people loathe all of them.

CHAPTER TWO

Longest Serving Heads of State in Africa and the Rest of the World

R a n k	Name	Country	Office	Tenure Began	Length of Tenure
1	Paul Biya	Cameroon	Prime Minister, then President	30 June 1975	43 Years
2	Teodoro Obiang Nguema Mbasogo	Equatorial Guinea	President[1]	3 August 1979	38 Years

3	Ali Khamenei	Iran	President, then Supreme Head	13 October 1981	36 Years
4	Denis Sassou Nguesso	Republic of Congo	President	25 October 1997	18 Years
5	Hun Sen	Cambodia	Prime Minister[2]	14 January 1985	33 Years
6	Yoweri Museveni	Uganda	President	29 January 1986	32 Years
7	Nursultan Nazarbayev	Kazakhstan	First Secretary, then President	22 June 1989	29 Years
8	Omar al-Bashir	Sudan	President[3]	30 June 1989	29 Years
9	Idriss Déby	Chad	President[4]	2 December 1990	27 Years

10	Isaias Afwerki	Eritrea	President[5]	27 April 1991	27 Years
11	Emomali Rahmon	Tajikistan	President	19 November 1992	25 Years
12	Paul Kagame	Rwanda	President	19 July 1994	24 Years
13	Alexander Lukashenko	Belarus	President	20 July 1994	24 Years
14	Milo Đukanović	Montenegro	Prime Minister, then President	02/15/1991-11/25/2002 and 01/08/2003-11/10/2006 and 02/29/2008-12/29/2010 and 05/20/2018–present	22 Years
15	Mahathir	Malaysia	Prime	07/16/1981-10/31/2003	22 Years

	Mohamad		Minister	and 05/10/2018 – present	
16	Daniel Ortega	Nicaragua	President	03/04/1981- 04/25/ 1990 and 01/10/2007 – present	20 Years
17	Tuilaepa Aiono Sailele Malielegaoi	Samoa	Prime Minister	23 November 1998	19 Years
17	Abdelaziz Bouteflika	Algeria	President	27 April 1999	19 Years
18	Ismaïl Omar Guelleh	Djibouti	President	8 May 1999	19 Years
19	Vladimir Putin	Russia	President[10]	9 August 1999	19 Years
20	Keith Mitchell	Grenada	Prime Minister	06/22/1995- 07/09 2008 and	18 Years

				02/20/2013-present	
21	Hage Geingob	Namibia	Prime Minister, then President	03/21/1990-08/28/2002 and 12/04/2012- – present	18 Years
22	Bashar al-Assad	Syria	President	17 July 2000	18 Years
23	Joseph Kabila	Congo, The Democratic Republic of	President	17 January 2001	17 Years
24	Ralph Gonsalves	Saint Vincent-and-the-Grenadines	Prime Minister	29 March 2001	17 Years
25	Barnabas Sibusiso Dlamini	Swaziland	Prime Minister	07/26/1996-09/29/ 2003 and 10/23/2008 – present	17 Years

26	Dési Bouterse	Surinam	President	02/25/1980- 01/25/ 1988 and 08/12/ 2010 – present	15 Years
27	Recep Tayyip Erdoğan	Turkey	Prime Minister, then President	14 March 2003	15 Years
28	Ilham Aliyev	Azerbaijan	Prime Minister, then President[12]	4 August 2003	15 Years
29	Shavkat Mirziyoyev	Uzbekistan	Prime Minister, then President	11 December 2003	14 Years
30	Sheikh Hasina	Bangladesh	Prime Minister	06/231996-07/ 15/ 2001 and 01/6 2009 – present	14 Years

31	Roosevelt Skerrit	Dominica	Prime Minister	8 January 2004	14 Years
32	Mahmoud Abbas	Palestine	Prime Minister, then President	03/19/2003-09/06/2003 01/15/2005 – present	12 Years
33	Lee Hsien Loong	Singapore	Prime Minister	12 August 2004	13 Years
34	Tommy Remengesau	Palau	President	01/01/2001-01/15/2009 and 01/17/ 2013 – present	13 Years
35	Faure Gnassingbé	Togo	President[15]	4 May 2005	13 Years
36	Salva Kiir Maiardit	South Sudan	President[16]	30 July 2005	13 Years
37	Pierre	Burundi	President	26 August	13 Years

	Nkurunziza			2005	
38	Angelina Merkel	Germany	Federal Chancellor	22 November 2005	12 Years
39	Evo Morales	Bolivia	President	22 January 2006	12 Years
40	Benjamin Netanyahu	Israel	Prime Minister	06/18/1996- 07/0 6/1999 and 03/31/ 2009 – present	12 Years
41	Viktor Orban	Hungary	Prime Minister	07/06/1998 – 05/27/2002 and 05/29/2010 – present	12 Years
41	Doris Leuthard	Switzerland	Member of the Federation Council, erstwhile	1 August 2006	11 Years

			President		
42	Frank Bainimarama	Fiji	Interim President, then Prime Minister	05/29/2000-07/13/ 2000 and 12/5/2006 – present	11 Years
43	Gurbanguly Berdimuham edow	Turkmenistan	President	21 December 2006	11 Years
44	Ibrahim Boubacar Keïta	Mali	Prime Minister, then President	02/04/1994-02/15/2000 and 09/04/2013 – present	10 Years
45	Bako Sahakyan	Artsakh (former Nagorno-Karabakh Autonomous Oblast)	President	7 September20 07	10 Years

46	Alassane Ouattara	Côte d'Ivoire	Prime Minister, then President	11/07/1990-11/9/ 1993 and 12/04/2010-present (2nd time)	10 Years
47	Dean Barrow	Belize	Prime Minister	8 February 2008	10 Years
48	Dmitry Medvedev	Russia	President, then Prime Minister	07 May 2008	10 Years

CHAPTER THREE

Politicians and Revolutionaries in the Struggle for the New Cameroon

Politicians are not those who are meant to change a system and take a country out of an impasse into the future. That is the work of revolutionaries.

Politicians operate in established systems and do the job of politicking to defend, safeguard or promote certain interests, be they individual, group, ethnic, regional, linguistic or national, based on empty phrases or through a clearly defined thought formulation (idea or concept).

Revolutionaries, on the other hand, are those challenging a system, expecting to bring it down and institute a new system that would serve the interest of the trodden majority (the suffering or struggling masses). in the cause to bring down the system, revolutionaries do not expect to benefit or thrive from the struggle. Instead, they are prepared to sacrifice everything for the struggle.

The sad thing is that while the Cameroonian struggle to change the system is a revolutionary struggle, most of the leadership in the so-called opposition parties talk of politics and expected rewards even though they are still engaged in the struggle to change the system. That is why most of them compromised the ideals of the struggle with excuses that "it is impossible to live on clean politics as a genuine opposition in Cameroon." There are and there have been Cameroonians who selflessly gave in their worth to the struggle and felt it was dishonorable to use the struggle to achieve personal benefits. They were and are the union-nationalists and revolutionaries.

During my years of involvement in the struggle, I finally realized that the system (the Ahidjo-Biya regimes backed by the French mafia group controlling African affairs) feared and respected these revolutionaries and union-nationalists for their genuineness, unwavering nature, and integrity. But strangely enough, the politicians who profess to be in the opposition conceived a hatred for these revolutionaries and union nationalists just because these revolutionaries and union nationalists are genuine and are not like them, and because they look with horror at the deception of the politicians who are trying to live off politicking and in doing so, compromised the struggle and betrayed the aspirations of the struggling masses.

Strangely enough, we failed in this phase of the struggle (1990-2002) because politicians led the struggle to change the system (a revolutionary demand) instead of revolutionaries and union-nationalists who are far less likely to be compromised by the negative values of the anachronistic French-imposed system.

Janvier Tchouteu   *Friday, 15 April 2005*

CHAPTER FOUR

PAUL BIYA, THE HEAD OF STATE OF CAMEROON:
The Living Specter that is Haunting Cameroonians

Pose this question to any Cameroonian with a deep perception of the world: Who is Africa's most dishonest and illusionary head of state? The answer from the absolute majority would be obvious. Our tenant in the unity palace is that head of state.

Cameroon's second president is a bad leader in the furthest sense of the word. His governance has destroyed most of the foundations of our people's way of life and progressive values. Unprincipled, unscrupulous and visionless, he was elusive enough during his early years of leadership by convincing many to regard him as a brilliant leader. Yes, he made himself brilliant and appealing to the people even despite his true convictions.

The second Cameroonian president as the demagogue he is, harangued about his NEW DEAL of Rigor and Moralization when he never intended to work for the interest of all Cameroonians. He came to power for the sole purpose of defending the interest of his patron (The mafia in the French establishment over its African policy), to enhance the material well-being and social position of his clique of unscrupulous businessmen, politicians, functionaries and above all the ethnic group of his birth.

A second Cameroonian president is a dishonorable man without convictions. He began his political manifestations as a

Cameroonian nationalist of socialist orientation under the banner of the Union of the Populations of Cameroon (UPC), but soon unhesitatingly discarded his nationalist garment for the high positions offered to renegades of the Cameroonian struggle by the Anglophobic Ahidjo regime and its French masters. Having switched his loyalty to the glory of naked power in the French-backed regime overseeing the genocide of the union-nationalist forces in Cameroon, Paul Biya quickly won the hearts of his patron to become prime minister in 1972 and later president in 1982. After that, he shed all aspects of his ties to Cameroonian nationalism and became a fervent Francophile and Anglophone manipulator. Today, it is clear for all to see that Paul Biya stands as the leader of the renegade forces that may eventually kill Cameroonian nationalism and lead the nation into the abyss, denying it the realization of its century-old Cameroonian dream of unity, independence, prosperity, and open opportunities. He is a purposeless, faceless and paranoiac leader whose long years of power and the emptiness of his rule have been masked by France and his Cameroonian collaborators.

During his early years as head of state, Paul Biya talked of rigor in the implementation of progressive work ethics, rules, laws, freedom, Human rights, and economic reforms, when he never intended to see the slightest change in the French imposed system he inherited from his predecessor. Biya never had any intention to change the course of dictatorship, corruption, kleptomania, and division that was the rule of the system and the trappings of power and wealth it offered. A decade after his pronouncement of rigor, Cameroon which had the second-fastest economic growth rate in the world after South Korea in 1986(though it lagged behind its true potentials even then), is today with the least promising economy in Africa.

Biya's moralization rhetoric is an unacceptable abuse to

humanity. Promising to make his rule a moral one where governance would be based on a program to enhance the right conducts in public, social, economic and political affairs, he reneged by presiding over the worst degeneration of a non-war-ravaged nation in Africa.

Unfortunately, for Cameroonians, Biya is one of those regrettable products of nature with quite an exceptional strength of character that is a negation of good leadership. It does not bother him in the least that his practically wrong actions and leadership have reduced Cameroonians into a poverty-stricken people, eroded their sense of purpose, divided their ranks, rendered them into the grips of despondence, denigrated their influence in national and international politics, and encouraged corruption to the form of art; and above all, it suits his propose that he has wrapped Cameroon into the clutch and whims of France.

After becoming the president in 1982, Biya has ruled Cameroon more like an absentee caretaker than even an absentee landlord. A two-month trip abroad for amusement using the taxpayer's money is unprecedented from any head of state. Nevertheless, it surprises only those who have no insight into his personality. Biya committed moral suicide years ago and now lacks the morality that is expected from a head of state. His rule has shattered the bilateral respect that prevailed between the different generations.

From peasant origins, Biya has learned but wrongly assimilated aristocratic values. The sad result of this is his blatant and unjustifiable contempt of the masses from where he had his origins. As a man of high learning, it is unfortunate that despite his long years of service in the system, he still possesses all the traits of a pseudo-intellectual and a pedant. And it is due to his awareness of his intellectual feebleness that he has developed a masked inferiority complex. That is why he rejects, snubs and shies away from the good ideas of his intellectual superiors.

Cameroon is the only nation in Africa where its true liberation fighters and nationalists were never permitted to the helm of power. It is the first nation in Africa where France became deeply involved in collaboration with Ahidjo, in the genocide of those who resisted its deception (close to a million deaths in the 1956-1970 war against the UPC). Cameroon is the only country in Africa, which has been the most cruelly raped in our modern times by France. Even though Cameroonians are one of the most dynamic people on the continent, they have never been left to their devices to harness their potentials and build their country into the great nation that it truly deserves. Instead, Cameroonians have been brought low by a conspiracy hatched during the years of Jacques Foccart's control of French policy on Africa, a conspiracy that has effectively used Cameroonian collaborators, especially Paul Biya.

It does not bother the second Cameroonian president in the least that the Cameroonian people are suffocating in his bondage. He has lost touch with the Cameroonian masses, the Cameroonian reality, and life in its different forms. However, unlike his psychopathic counterpart, the Roman emperor Nero, he has mastered one art—the art of retaining power despite the opposition from the masses. And as most megalomaniacs and experimentalists, he would continue to experiment with his theory of power retention, despite his unpopularity, not worried that the Cameroonian people are being dragged into the abyss in the process.

Biya is performing his theory of power retention on us, an experiment that will go a long way to destroy the best of our creative forces if left to persist. Moreover, with that will be the destruction of the faith we have in our dream and worst still the mother of progress, which is hope. The sad result of the disaster of Biya's rule would be the death of Cameroon. To the rational mind, that is unacceptable.

Perhaps for a little while longer, the living specter of the second Cameroonian president will continue to haunt the people—treacherous in his ways, ruthless in his methods and nonchalant in his views. It is our unavoidable task, if only for the sake of our children, that we rise up—take back our dignity, hope and future from him and his patrons. Then following the natural course of history, we shall confine him and his legacy to the dustbin of history.

February 28, 1995   *Janvier Tchouteu*

CHAPTER FIVE

Africa's Haunted Heart

A specter looms in the lives of every Cameroonian child, man or woman. It is the living president of the land in the middle of Africa, the land that is often referred to as the microcosm of the continent. The specter is President Paul Biya of Cameroon. When rumors spread like wildfire in June 2004 that he had just died, there were widespread scenes of jubilation all across the half a million square kilometer landmass called Cameroon. Days after the circulation of the unverified account, he returned home from abroad where he had been passing his time, intermittently, about six months every year for over two decades, and then declared to the sycophants waiting to receive him at the airport that there would be a .... "Rendez-vous in 20 years' time with those who wish me dead..."

Cameroonians were not the only ones who disbelieved him when he made that pronouncement among other things. Many of those who follow political developments in the world in general, and in Africa and Cameroon in particular, marveled at his audacity. After all, more than 80% of the Cameroonian population loathed his rule; he was already in power for more than two decades as the head of state, after having been the country's prime minister (1972-1982) or the second most powerful person in the system put in place in Cameroon by the French overlords.

But Paul Biya proved everyone wrong. He pulled off another electoral charade and declared himself the winner in the October 2004 presidential election, and then changed his constitution in 2008 that would allow him to run for two more presidential 7-year terms (despite the deaths of 150 protesting Cameroonians caused by his armed forces), meaning that he could be president until the year 2025 (a record of 43 years in power) when he would be 92 years of age.

That explains why by the time Paul Biya held another masquerade called presidential elections in October 2011, he had already successfully humbled the internationally recognized opposition heads (who are all former members of the country's sole political party from 1972-1990, a party Biya has been leading since 1984), promised to give them positions in his government and made it known in plain terms that the system string-controlled by the puppeteer (France) would never allow a political change in Cameroon that would curtail France's unrestricted interests in the African country.

The octogenarian Paul Biya is variously described as the Maradona (he fakes and wins elections just like Maradona faked and scored a goal in his "Hand of God" goal) of Cameroonian and African politics, the master of presidential patricide (he devoured his predecessor who handed power over to him, leading to the first Cameroonian president Ahmadou Ahidjo's exile, death and burial abroad—Senegal), the absentee president, the vindictive president, the evil president, etc. etc.

As a German colony from 1884-1916, Kamerun was often referred to by the German Colonial administration and the imperial-minded in the Kaiser's Germany as an "African Pearl", owing to the colony's robust economy, the highest literacy rate in the continent in the early 1900s, magnificent physical features, rich and varied vegetation cover, and also owing to its diverse ethnic ethnicities that included all the major language groups in Africa (Afro-Asia, Niger-Congo-A, Niger-Congo-B or Bantu, and Nilo-Saharan. In fact, historians consider the German colony of Kamerun as a major part of Adolf Hitler's rue over the territories Germany lost after the First World because of the peace terms imposed on it by the victories Allied Powers during the Versailles Conference. As it happens, one of the peace terms imposed on the post-Kaiser Germany was the loss of German Kamerun to Britain and France. That was how Kamerun was partitioned into British Cameroons and French Cameroon.

As a matter of fact, the French Cameroun mandate became France's most valuable assets in Sub-Saharan Africa. Its value was validated even further when the territory became the Launchpad of French General Charles De Gaulle-led Free French Forces that wrestled French Equatorial Africa from the Nazi puppet regime of Vichy France during the Second World War. This force would gallantly fight alongside Allied Forces against Italian and German forces in Libya, Tunisia and the Middle East, before carrying on to Italy and France, where their biggest achievement was the liberation of Paris. The fact that French Camerounians played an invaluable role in the war effort to liberate France from Nazi Germany makes the explanation simple as to why French Camerounian soldiers returned home and sought self-government, liberty, democracy, reunification with British Cameroons that would culminate in the independence of the two United Nations Trust Territories. They were merely seeking the rights that they had helped France to regain from Nazi Germany, which is why pundits were not surprised at all.

The formation of the UPC (Union of the Populations of the Camerouns) in French Cameroun in 1946 and the birth of sister union-nationalist (civic-nationalist) parties in British Cameroons highlighted the seriousness of the former Kamerunians to work together to build a "New Cameroon". By 1955, the UPC commanded more than 80% of popular support in French Cameroun.

So pundits considered it foolhardy when the French government issued a decree banning the UPC on July 13, 1955, in French Cameroons, a strategic act that was followed by the party's ban in British Cameroons three years later on the same fabricated charges of inciting violence and for being communists. These coordinated moves by Africa's two foremost colonial masters at the time were supposed to spell disaster for the dream held by Cameroon's leaders. Many Cameroonians saw nothing but duplicity and hypocrisy in the moves, wondering whether the freedom they had assisted the Free French Forces to achieve for France and its citizens was a special right or privilege meant for "White People" only.

When in 1956, the UPC resorted to a partisan war of liberation from French rule, it was a belated move to confront France after failing to resolve the ban in a peaceful manner. That war would end with the defeat of the UPC in 1970, a defeat that came with the assassinations and execution of the party's successive heads in 1958, 1960 and 1971, i.e., the deaths of Ruben Um Nyobè, Dr. Felix Moumié, and Ernest Ouandié respectively. It would leave Cameroon entrapped through a French-imposed system rooted in the Colonial Pact France made its puppets sign before allowing their countries to become members of the United Nations Organization by granting these former colonies string-controlled independence.

Despite the period of instability during the country's unsuccessful war of liberation that saw the French Trusteeship masters handing power to those who never asked for or never fought for it (the puppets that constitute the system today), despite the eventual peaceful reunification of British Southern Cameroons with former French Cameroun, despite Cameroon's agricultural recovery and the discovery of oil in the 1970s that saw the country emerge as Africa's eighth-largest economy and the world's second-fastest-growing in the early 1980s, Cameroon is today in a horrible shape.

The Cameroonian economy that was expected to grow twenty times over the next thirty years, i.e., from 1982-2012, barely doubled over that period. Everything changed for the worse after Paul Biya was handed power in November 1982 by the first French-installed puppet Cameroonian president Ahmadou Ahidjo. Since then, Cameroon has experienced the biggest proportionate embezzlement of state funds ever recorded in Africa. And the country holds the sad record as the country in Africa that has experienced the worst peacetime impoverishment since 1960.

Today, President Paul Biya is presiding over a nation where more than 80% of its physicians are abroad, where more than 90% of its doctorate degree holders are abroad, where Cameroonians invest abroad more than at home, where Cameroonians are voting against the system with their feet; today, Cameroon's neighbors who before envied its high standards of living and saw it as a place of refuge and opportunities, now find Cameroonians envying them as they forge ahead with a sense of direction while Cameroon lags behind in its spiral towards total, complete and horrifying economic, social and political decay.

People unfamiliar with the Cameroonian situation would be wondering why such an abysmal situation persists. Well; the answer is simple. Cameroon finds itself today in a situation like someone in quicksand because of the anachronistic system put in place by Gaullist France when General Charles De Gaulle returned to power in 1958 and decided to make France's former colonies and territories members of the United Nations Organization (UNO), while controlling them with transparent or invisible strings this time. French Cameroun and British Southern Cameroons achieved independence and reunification all right, only for the people to find that the new country is quasi-independent under a broader French template of control variously described as FrancAfrique. This French-imposed system has traumatized, demoralized, divided and dehumanized the Cameroonian people over the years.

The Gaullist system put in place by the elites of the French political establishment has as one of its major objectives the exclusion from Cameroon's political power of the union-nationalists advocating for the reunification and independence of the divided territories of the former German Kamerun, civic nationalists who commanded the support of more than 80% of the populations of both territories of British Cameroons and French Cameroun in the 1950s and 1960s. The current system in Cameroon is a partnership of French imperial interest in Africa (economic and political) otherwise known as FrancAfrique and its Cameroonian collaborators (the renegades and anti-union-nationalists who never opposed and who do not object to France's neo-colonial stranglehold of Cameroon).

The system has been effective in infecting the minds of many Cameroonians, reducing them into a state of hopelessness, in a process that lures them to direct their energy not against the Biya regime and the system, but at their neighbors. The system has successfully elevated corruption and the divide-and-rule strategy into an art—it has promoted the notion of settlers and indigenes, it has encouraged ethnocentrism, tribalism, clannishness, regional jingoism, sectarianism and other forms of division. We see a total and complete absence of strategic or even tactical planning when it comes to the economic and social development of the nation. We see a complete absence of social solidarity.

To compound the division and confusion among the people who

reject the Biya regime and the French-imposed system, the so-called opposition leaders these freedom-craving Cameroonians had been looking up to have now been absorbed back into the system, leaving the struggling Cameroonian masses distrustful of politicians in general. Today, the down-trodden Cameroonian people are in a state of political lethargy.

When Paul Biya called for the holding of Senate elections in April 2013, eighteen years after his parliament promulgated a law to create one, most Cameroonians thought it would be another charade, as usual. It made no sense for the so-called opposition parties with a semblance of representation in parliament to glorify the charade with their participation. Most Cameroonians knew the system was sustaining these so-called opposition leaders financially and that some of them were in the government, but Cameroonians were not prepared for the extent to which these politicians would go to insult their intelligence. But deals between the ruling party and the opposition were made all right. The electoral masquerade took place and the people saw the ruling party campaigning for the so-called main opposition party (Social Democratic Front—SDF) in some regions of the country, while the SDF in the words of its chairman or president John Fru Ndi "…one good turn deserves another…", openly backed the ruling party, thereby ensuring its victory in other regions of the country.

How could that have happened? Politically-shocked Cameroonians have been asking themselves ever since the open fornication between the ruling party and the so-called opposition political parties in April 2013.

To prevent chaos and ensure a smooth succession, SDF spokespersons, and apologists quip.

"Paul Biya has a deal with the SDF to hand over power to one of its members," some anonymous voices within the SDF echo.

If you ask me, my answer is clear. What was supposed to be a

Cameroonian revolution that began on May 26, 1990, became a political comedy played by former members of the French-imposed system or political establishment, a political comedy that has gone full circle. The worldwide wind of change generated by Mikhail Gorbachev's Glasnost and Perestroika that swept away authoritarian systems in Eastern Europe and Africa, and that stirred the vast majority of Cameroonians in the 1990s to risk their lives in the streets demanding political change, was effectively controlled by the system. The desire for change that more than 80% of Cameroonians have has been hijacked by the authoritarian system in Cameroon and the so-called leaders of the opposition. The people got taken for a ride.

The biggest mistake made by Cameroonians was that when the clamor for change began, they followed Cameroonians who had no democratic credentials, people who hardly a year before, were in the upper echelons of power in the system, but who at the time claimed they had left the ruling party and now opposed it. All the so-called heads of what the world knows today as the prominent opposition parties in Cameroon (John Fru Ndi of the SDF, Bello Bouba Maigari of the UNDP, Adamou Ndam Njoya of the CDU etc.) were members of the ruling party right up to the year 1990, when the system was forced to accept multi-party politics in Cameroon. Like the Pied Piper, these so-called opposition leaders lured freedom-starved Cameroonians into greater despondency and political lethargy. Such a feat was achieved only because Cameroonian liberals, union-nationalists, revolutionaries, democrats and patriots who had always rejected the system, thought these so-called heads of the so-called new opposition, these people who were the first to make the moves to create political parties, shared the vision of the "New Cameroon" that Cameroonians fought, died and voted for, a vision that achieved the land's reunification and independence (though it has never been real because it got usurped by the evil system that today is under the leadership of Paul Biya and his French puppeteers.), but that is yet to realize democracy, freedom, liberalism, progress, justice, equality and development.

False are the statements by members of the compromised opposition that had they not openly embraced the Biya regime and the system, chaos would have ensued in Cameroon in case Biya exited the political scene. There is no truth in the statement because the system in Cameroon is authoritarian, not autocratic.

Authoritarian regimes are usually coated with a sublime idea that could be political (Stalinism/Marxism/Communism, Fascism etc.), that could be religious (Iranian and Taliban theocracy etc.) or that could be an interest arrangement (FrancAfrique). In Cameroon, the system is built on a framework of using compradors to maintain France's lopsided interest in Cameroon and around preventing those who believe in the Cameroonian struggle (the union-nationalists, otherwise called the Kamerunists) from attaining power and working for the realization of the NEW CAMEROON that has been the original Cameroonian dream for over a century.

The system in Cameroon is a collection of individual interest groups, bringing together the propagators of French neo-colonialism and their Cameroonian collaborators. Paul Biya is the head of the collaborationists. And in many ways, he has been acting over the years as an absentee president. Meanwhile, the state has been functioning zombie-like during his quasi-presence. As a matter of fact, even though the mortifying arrangement suited the interest of the puppeteers and the beneficiaries of the system, it exposed the system to popular uprisings since that means the beneficiaries of the system are not clearly or functionally organized. With the advent of social media, globalization, the maturity of post-independence generations that never benefited from the system; and with the soldiers of the 1990s phase of the struggle dissociating themselves from the so-called opposition leaders, the authoritarian system now finds itself even more vulnerable.

The authoritarian system would be faced by a new political force that never associated itself with the system, a new political force that embodies the spirit of the century-old struggle for the "NEW KAMERUN" or "NEW CAMEROON" that confronted German colonial control, stood up to French duplicity in the land in a war that decimated more than half a million of its supporters; the authoritarian system would be faced by a new force that embraces the legacy of those who fought, died and voted for the independence and reunification of Cameroon, a new force that rejects all the values of the system that the French political mafia over Africa put in place in their game plan to control the destiny of Cameroon, a six-decade-old evil system that can only lead the country to abyss.

Now, as the open and hidden collaborators of the system openly embrace one another (the ruling party and the so-called heads of the so-called opposition parties) starting with the recent senatorial charade where the so-called principal opposition—the Social Democratic Front (SDF) and the party of Paul Biya—Cameroon People's Democratic Movement (CPDM) supported each other's aspirations in agreed-upon provinces with guaranteed votes from party members, the system is encouraging the creation of elite groups of beneficiaries who see or think that their political and economic survival rests only in a continuation or sustenance of the system. We are observing the evolvement of a system that is shedding any pretense of limited political pluralism; we are observing the entrenchment of a system that openly views the people as its number one enemy. Such a system then becomes autocratic.

In a nutshell, Cameroon's so-called opposition political parties that are in symbiosis with the authoritarian system are aiding the system in its gradual transition into an autocratic system, thereby ensuring its survival in a morphed form. The rapidly changing system needs a strong man to be truly autocratic. This would be someone who has the hands-on experience to act as the president, someone who the French puppeteers would like to portray as the benevolent despot.

As Egyptian writer Alaa Al -Aswany said, "The concept of the benevolent dictator, just like the concepts of the noble thief or the honest whore, is no more than a meaningless fantasy."

It is the place of post-independence Cameroonians to reject whatever farce the system comes up with as change whenever power passes down to the generation after Paul Biya. By absorbing former members of his party who for decades identified with the opposition, Biya is trying to give Cameroonians and the rest of the world the impression that Cameroon's opposition is in sync with his vision for the political evolution of Cameroon. Unfortunately, the system does not intend to let the majority of Cameroonians participate or have a say in Cameroon's political development or evolution.

The New Cameroon will be founded. Not by beneficiaries of the system (past and present) but by those who have always rejected it as an evil system that has been leading Cameroon into the abyss.

But then, in founding the New Cameroon, patriotic, honest, democratic, unbiased and progressive-minded Cameroonians would have to reconcile a country where:

- the system made sure that most of its historic figures who dedicated their lives and even died for the cause for Cameroon's reunification and independence got killed and buried like dogs at home and abroad,

- the bodies of some of these historic figures that got buried abroad are missing,
- a few of the historic figures who thought they could contribute to nation-building got sidelined, cowed and humiliated by the system,
- its first head of state died and is buried abroad,
- and where the people have been insulted for more than five decades by the regimes of Ahmadou Ahidjo and Paul Biya through an imposed minority system that sowed the seeds of division, corruption, mediocrity, fear, and despondency that are haunting Cameroon today.

The ideas and ideals of the New Cameroon hatched by the country's historic civic-nationalists and developed over the years by post-independence union-nationalists is Cameroon's only bargain with the future. It is the only nucleus around which Cameroon can reconcile with its turbulent past; it is the nucleus that all the strata of Cameroonian society can connect to in the process of nation-building; it is the only nucleus around which a free, democratic, liberal, fair and prosperous Cameroon can be built. The New Cameroon would lead the country in taking its merited place in the central African region, Africa as a whole, and the world at large. That would be possible only if we confine the legacies of the Ahidjo/Biya regimes and the suffocating French-imposed system to the dustbin of history.

Janvier Tchouteu   *06/04/2013*

CHAPTER SIX

The Logic-Defying Land: Paul Biya and the Franco-Cameroonian Political Mafia that keeps him in Power

A close monitoring of Cameroonian and world economic trends over the past three decades has revealed an unadulterated and persistent fact that no conscientious person, African, Cameroonian, altruist or otherwise would be indifferent about after it has been brought to his/her attention. Over the past five decades, the French-imposed system has brought what was once Africa's most promising land to its knees and eroded its sense of direction, putting it in the grips of despondence and the worst mafia the continent has ever experienced.

Cameroon's GDP over the decades has shown that the Biya regime is the only governing entity in the world "that becomes popular and wins elections with landslides whenever the national economy is in a recession". The chutzpah of the Biya regime defies logic to the point where the administration manufactures victories in elections even at a time that Cameroon is ranked as the world's most corrupt country.

Considering the decades of inflation, the more than doubling of the national population, etc., what becomes evident is that the average Cameroonian is living on less than thirty percent (30%) of the real GDP per capita of his compatriot two and a half decades ago. Poverty is rife today than it was before independence. Moreover, we are one of the few countries in Africa and the world that has no sense of direction. The reasons are obvious. The system is anachronistic. It is a fake structure of clay that cannot be reformed. It promises only doom.

Legislative and Presidential Elections in Cameroon since the Return of Multi-party Politics in 1990

Election Type/Year	Paul Biya's "% Win"?	Ruling Party (CPDM) "No of Seats--- %Win"	Number of Candidates or Parties with Seats
Parliamentary Election, 1992		88 Seats (45.5 %)	4
Presidential Election, 1992	40%		6
Parliamentary Election, 1997		109 Seats (61%)	7
Presidential Election, 1997	92.57%		7
Parliamentary Election, 2002		149 Seats (83%)	5
Presidential Election, 2004	70.92%		16
Parliamentary Election, 2007		153 Seats (85%)	5
Presidential Election, 2011	77.99%		23

Cameroon GDP between 1980-2017 ($1,000): Real and estimates by the IMF. Cameroon Gross Domestic Product (GDP) between 1980-2017 ($1,000,000): Real and estimates by the IMF. Cameroon Gross Domestic Product (GDP) between 1980-2017 ($1,000,000): Real and estimates by the IMF.

Country	1980	1981	1982	1983	1984	1985	1986	1987	1988	1989
Cameroon	7,649	8,665	8,310	8,376	8,853	9,246	12,052	13,960	14,176	12,640

Country	1990	1991	1992	1993	1994	1995	1996	1997	1998	1999
Cameroon	12,654	14,109	12,931	13,492	8,912	9,036	10,335	10,343	9,875	10,424

Country	2000	2001	2002	2003	2004	2005	2006	2007	2008	2009
Cameroon	10,046	9,497	10,888	13,630	15,784	16,593	17,957	20,433	23,732	22,194

Country	2010	2011	2012	2013	2014	2015	2016	2017
Cameroon	22,468	25,759	25,538	27,482	29,283	31,137	33,258	35,596

Paul Biya, the head of state of Cameroon who was schemed onto power by French President Francois Mitterrand of France in 1982 after the Frenchman manipulated the former Cameroonian president Ahmadou Ahidjo into handing power to Biya, who at the time, was Ahidjo's prime minister, has been making himself the winner of pseudo-elections aimed at renewing his presidential mandate. He organizes this charade of fake elections to legitimize his rule, something his Western backers (puppet masters) validate by recognizing his victory in these sham election. Is he blind to the fact that the world knows he is loathed by the Cameroonian people; or is it an extreme case of chutzpah as he grants to himself higher percentages of victory in every following election even though the economy has been declining in a persistent manner, especially vis-a-vis the economies of neighboring countries and the rest of Africa?

In a nutshell, the population of Cameroon has more than tripled since Paul Biya became the head of state in 1982, but the Gross Domestic Product has not even quadrupled. And taking account of inflation which has more than quadrupled over the years, we see that under Paul Biya, the standard of living of Cameroonians has dropped and their real purchasing power and per capita income has reduced by more than half.

Election years are highlighted in yellow.

Saturday, June 11, 2016   *Janvier Tchouteu*

PART TWO

Cameroon and
Anglophone Cameroon's
(Southern Cameroon's)
Irredentism

CHAPTER SEVEN

Cameroon's Unity and the Hopes, Dreams, and Fears of the Kamerunists (Union-Nationalists of Cameroon)

The union nationalists of Cameroon are pragmatic revolutionists, progressive reformers or radical evolutionists. These are men and women who grew up being what they are more as a confection of circumstance than of what was bestowed upon them by birth that gave them a social identity. These people greatly developed or did not suppress their human touch. Unlike most, they do not find it easy to live without the slightest spasm over the pains and suffering of their fellow compatriots. Unlike most, they have put their purposes far above personal considerations and even above their personal interest, an uncommon quality. By dwelling on their sense of humanity, they consider the alleviation of the pains, turmoil, and nightmares of their compatriots over the alleviation of their personal well-being. It is because of their all-embracing humanitarianism and the depth of their awareness of the Cameroonian reality that they accepted the fact that the demanding task of alleviation cannot be based on individuals who are so many and complex as separate entities. Cameroon's union-nationalists are acutely aware of the fact that the task of alleviation should be for the entire Cameroonian people. They know that Cameroonians have been dishonored, oppressed and traumatized en-mass and not separately.

Permit me to call Cameroon's union-nationalists the advanced Cameroonians. These exceptional groups of patriots, who have been shaped by circumstance and have a clear sense of the meaning of life, have never been allowed to the helm of power in the country's political life. With legendary origins and gruesome pasts, they are the best reflection of Cameroon itself. Cameroon's union-nationalists are aware of tribal, ethnic, religious, cultural and linguistic sentiments; however, they have not allowed these to blind and overwhelm their reasoning for a progressive Cameroon. They are aware of the fact that Cameroon's chronic malady lies in its anachronistic institutions, complete dominance by France and a detached oligarchic leadership. It is the different sentiments and workings of the French-imposed system that has shaped individual Cameroonians to varying degrees and constrains them in their drive towards authentic change and progress. However, Cameroon's union-nationalists in their advanced ideals are those exceptional compatriots who have detached themselves from the shortcomings of the system and the blinding sentiments of tribal, ethnic, religious, cultural, linguistic and social ties. They stand as the epitome of the renewed Cameroonian.

Since becoming a distinctive entity under the German colonial rule eleven decades ago, Cameroon has occasionally conceived of liberation movements that would have advanced the nation into a better position had these civic-nationalist forces been successful in their cause.

In 1910, Martin Paul Samba (Mebenga Mebono), the first Kamerunian civic-nationalist leader realized that the progress and glory of the land rested more in a future that was devoid of colonial control and permeated by progressive Cameroonian concepts. He began one of the earliest liberation movements in Africa and the first in black Africa. However, time and fate cut him short in his campaign to rally the full support of the peoples of Kamerun. Cornered by the German colonial army near Ebolowa in 1914, he opted for surrender rather than face the massacre of his people. On August 8, 1914, Martin Paul Samba was executed, a day after the execution of his close friend and ally in the name of Rudolf Duala Manga Bell. That was the first trauma to Cameroonian civic-nationalism in the hands of the German colonial army, leading to defeat in the first phase of the Kamerunian struggle and to dormancy for its nationalism for years to come. It was such a deep trauma that even after British and French forces defeated the German army in Kamerun in 1916, no civic-nationalist force emerged to defend the territory from partition by the victorious European powers.

This partition into British Cameroons and French Cameroun, and the ensuing mandatory rule unfolded consequences of a disruption of past economic, political and cultural ties, as well as their resultant usage. Moreover, it is the shortcomings of partition and the disruptions that are haunting Cameroon's unity today. The imposition of separate English and French administrations in the land as agreed in the Mandate Formula only created systems that had little in common with pre-colonial experiences and that were out of touch with Cameroonian reality at the time.

Yes, it was due to the regrettable partition that Cameroon's civic-nationalism was rekindled three decades after, with a union content this time around in its quest to reunite British Cameroons and French Cameroun. It began in French Cameroun in 1948 under the UPC (Union of the populations of Cameroon) and spread over into British Cameroun where OK ((One Kamerun) and the KNDP (Kamerun National Democratic Party) championed it. The goals of both the English and French-speaking union-nationalists in the 1950s were to reunite the two territories and pursue the ultimate Cameroonian dream. The New Cameroon was envisaged to:

- Build a genuine bilingual ethos.
- Bridge the gap in the development of the English and French-speaking sectors.
- Work for the evolution of a New Cameroonian people from the different breeds of thoughts and actions of its francophone and Anglophone children.
- And create a democratic, liberal, free, progressive, united, strong and developed Kamerunian nation.

Leading exponents of this Cameroonian dream were Ruben Um Nyobè, Felix Moumié, Abel Kingué, Ernest Ouangie, Leonard Bouli, Etienne Libai, Osende Afana, Nde Ntumazah, and John Ngu Foncha. The majority of Cameroonians looked up to those legends of their times in the struggle to realize the Cameroonian dream propounded by Martin Paul Samba.

Imagine what Cameroon would have been today had its liberation fighters and union-nationalists been allowed to their devices to build the post-independence Cameroon. That was never the case. France was determined never to let go of its control of Cameroon, its African pearl. The French imposition of the system that persists in Cameroon today, and the installation of the puppet Ahidjo regime concretized the French plot that preceded the banning of the UPC in 1955.

This ruthless ten-year war to eliminate all aspects of UPC influence in the country, a genocidal campaign that saw the deaths of close to a million Cameroonians in the hands of French and Ahidjo forces resulted in an effective defeat of Cameroon's union-nationalists in the second phase of the Cameroonian struggle for independence, democracy, enlightenment, progress, and development. Ruben Um Nyobè, Felix-Roland Moumié, Osende Afana, Ernest Ouandié and several others in the UPC leadership were eliminated and the rest were either hounded into exile or cowed into capitulation by the French military and the puppet regime they put in place in Cameroon under Ahmadou Ahidjo. It was the death, the exile, and the capitulation of the heads of the second phase of the Cameroon Struggle and the smug complacency of the Cameroonian people that began Cameroon's infantile malady, a malady that has replaced hopes from a dream with fear and despair instead.

Imagine what Cameroon would have become had Anglophone and francophone union-nationalists realized its reunification, independence, and governance. Had that been the case, the following would have happened:

- The New Cameroon would have been born with an authentic and firm foundation.
- Cameroonians would have realized most of the union dreams (the objectives of reunification and independence).
- And in no way would the pressing legacies of partition still be as glaring as they are today.
- The continuation of the UPC liberation war against the persistent French army in Cameroon and the post-independence Cameroonian army of Francophiles(pseudo-nationalists) would have been avoided.
- Then the deaths of close to a million Cameroonians in the hands of Ahidjo and French troops would not have happened, a nightmarish genocide that still haunts Cameroonians. Those deaths imbued Cameroonians with a sense of skepticism, cynicism, despondency, treachery, dishonesty, and self-centeredness; and traumatized them into a state of political lethargy.

Today, most Cameroonians agree that the human obstacles to

nation-building lie more in the fact that reunification and independence were achieved by good-intentioned Anglophone union-nationalists and a Francophile Ahidjo regime that had little respect and knowledge of Anglophone aspirations and the collective Cameroonian dream (the objectives of reunification and independence). Ahidjo was put in power to defend the interest of those in the French political establishment, his collaborators and his ego. He was prepared to do that at all cost. Yes, it is this legacy of power retention, oppression, and division that the Biya regime inherited and is excessively, shamelessly and madly strengthening in order to maintain his hold onto power. Yes, the shameful Ahidjo regime betrayed the dream of reunification and independence and conceived of the virus of distrust, disintegration, and dishonesty that the Biya regime has proliferated to suffocate the cherished Cameroonian nation-state. This is a virus that has almost eroded our dynamic spirit and progressive values, leaving us with the looming specter of despondency, which threatens to doom Cameroon.

The reunification spirit and its all-embracing dream were the dominant factors in our political lives before the quasi-independence/reunification of the land. Nevertheless, it was the Anglophone community led by English-speaking union-nationalists who realized reunification. The role of Anglophone union-nationalists is the most patriotic to have been realized and the entire force of Cameroon's Union-Nationalism holds the people of the former British Southern Cameroons highly for that. Still, the ultimate Cameroonian dream, which is the responsibility of both English-speaking and French-speaking Cameroonians, has not been realized. The responsibility for that setback lies entirely with the French political establishment, Francophile regimes of Ahidjo and Biya, and their Anglophone collaborators. The unfortunate thing is that the Anglophone community has been the most betrayed. However, we must be honest with ourselves by accepting the fact that the entire Cameroonian people have been betrayed by the French-imposed system and that in our different ways, we too contributed to the success of the French-imposed regimes.

Today, it is getting to five years since the resurgence of Cameroon's union-nationalism. However, the years of lethargy still haunt the Cameroonian people. The questions now are:

- Must we allow the Cameroonian dream to die?
- Must we allow the realistic beliefs of the majority of Cameroonians for almost a century to end up as an illusion because France and its accomplices of unpatriotic and anti-nationalists Cameroonians do not cherish them?
- Must we allow Cameroon to disintegrate and fail the drive for reunification that was given a positive response in the 1961 plebiscite by British Southern Cameroonians, and gallantly fought for by the majority of former French-Camerounians, just because a treacherous minority that constitutes the French-imposed establishment does not care?
- Must we allow despair to overwhelm our century-old dream and us?
- Should we betray our fallen legends and heroes because the price for rejecting the French-imposed system is too high?

No, the union-nationalists of Cameroon would not. They would not betray their ancestors, their dream, their heroes, their history of resistance and themselves.

Cameroonians would not surrender to despondency. They would continue the struggle against the oppressive and exploitative political influences in Cameroon in the guise of the current system. They would continue relentlessly in the struggle to eliminate the destructive aspects of the years of partition and Ahidjo-Biya rules.

Cameroonians would never surrender in the struggle against the anachronistic French-imposed system and the Biya regime. They are determined to continue in the struggle to eradicate the disheartening despair, division, cynicism, dishonesty and self-centeredness that have gripped the once noble Cameroonian soul. That is the will of the union-nationalists.

They are determined to continue hoisting the flag of the Cameroonian struggle to a logical conclusion. That commitment is not a matter of words. It is a difficult, demanding and selfless struggle—a task demanding actions, sacrifices and steadfastness. If we all get out of our lethargy and join the cause, all would soon be won; and we would not regret that we failed to save our nation from disintegration. That can be achieved only after we have discarded our self-centered attitudes and banish the negative legacies of partition and Ahidjo-Biya rules to the dustbin of history.

November 4, 1994   *Janvier   Tchouteu*

CHAPTER EIGHT

Cameroon's No 1 Minority Problem

No matter how Cameroon's inescapable problem is presented by its advocates, no matter whom these advocates direct their fire at, no matter how honorable or dishonorable some of the advocates for a solution of the inescapable problem are, no matter what the cause (difficult to define because of its diverse goals) promises upon its realization, the truth is that the number one minority problem in Cameroon is the predicament of the peoples west of the River Mungo (Southwestern German Kamerun, British Southern Cameroons, West Cameroon, Northwest and Southwest provinces, or what is today Northwest and Southwest regions). The problem was caused by the ill will or bad faith of the evil French-imposed system (the Ahidjo-Biya regimes of Cameroonians who did not support the reunification and independence cause), exacerbated by the docility and incomprehension of Cameroonians after their defeat by the evil system; but the problem would be solved by Cameroonians on both sides of the River Mungo working together to get rid of our living nightmare (the Biya regime and the evil system).

No linguistic entity (Francophones or Anglophones, or the different ethnic groups) is responsible for the plight of the peoples west of the River Mungo. The evil minority system supported by less than 10% of Cameroonians; a system that is rejected by every single ethnic group, province and religion in Cameroon; a system led today by Paul Biya in collaboration with criminals from every ethnic group, province, linguistic entity and religion; is what is suffocating the peoples west of the River Mungo and the rest of Cameroonians in general.

It is along those parameters that we, Cameroonians, can found the New Cameroon where all the grievances of its diverse peoples can be redressed. We can only realize that by closing ranks as victims of an evil system we never opted for.

Saturday, June 11, 2016   *Janvier Tchouteu*

CHAPTER NINE

What is the Anglophone Cameroonian Identity?

After watching a debate featuring the redoubtable Cameroonian journalist Franklin Sone Bayen and Joshua Osih (The Vice President of the Social Democratic Front), with the two facing off a host of French-speaking (Francophone) Cameroonian panelists, I could not help but come out disheartened by a fundamental fact—These Cameroonian patriots, Cameroonian civic-nationalists of Anglophone Cameroonian identify who deplore the system's handling of Cameroon, especially its treatment of the land and populations West of the River Mungo (The Northwest and Southwest regions or what was formerly West Cameroon and before that the British Trust Territory of Southern Cameroons, and what was down the line the Southwestern part of German Kamerun), apparently could not be understood in their brilliant presentation of the Anglophone Cameroonian problem. And what was even more disheartening was the fact that most of their learned counterparts were off the mark so many times and even went off on-the-tangent on the grievances of Cameroonians West of the River Mungo.

The New Cameroon would be able to resolve Cameroon's fundamental problems, that's for sure, fundamental problems of which the Anglophone Cameroonian problem is Number 1. But then, what is the Anglophone Cameroonian identity that the other panelists failed to get?

In a nutshell, what binds Anglophone Cameroonians together is something akin to a national identity, an emotional feeling of being a part of the geopolitical entity that is the Southwest and the Northwest regions of Cameroon (the former British Southern Cameroons and the former West Cameroon), a special feeling that arose from sharing a common history, a common language (pidgin English/English), a unique/similar culture, and a sense of marginalization. This sense of belonging, subjective as it may appear, is nurtured by Anglophone Cameroonians grounded on their ancestral ties to the area, or their native ties (having been born in either the Northwest and Southwest), and/or from growing up there from quite a young age, ignorant or hardly/barely conscious of any other identity. A person born and raised in Bangante, Yaoundé, Douala, Mbouda, Edea, Banyo and other towns of former East Cameroon (French-speaking region) and who studies in English these places, may not develop that Anglophone Cameroonian consciousness or feeling of belonging. This Anglophone Cameroonian identity does not hinder a person from being a Cameroonian Union-Nationalist (Cameroonian civic-nationalists). in fact, most Anglophone Cameroonians and most Francophone Cameroonians are Union-Nationalists, unlike the pseudo-nationalists that make up the political establishment (The CPDM elites and the elites of the so-called opposition—SDF, UNDP, CDU etc.) in Cameroon today, the French-imposed system stirred yesterday by the Ahidjo regime and today by the Biya regime; a system that has collaborators from all the religions, ethnic groups or tribes, regions of the country. And in fact, the Anglophone Cameroonians who want a separate state for the land West of the River Mungo are a minority.

Cameroonians should not be alarmed by the protesters in the

streets of Buea, Bamenda and other towns and cities of the Northwest and Southwest regions. They are the unsilenced voices of patriotic Cameroonians who reject the French-imposed system, the Biya regime and their perception of Cameroonians as a people that cannot set themselves free from tyranny. Cameroonians from other parts of the country should echo this voice of protest and resuscitate the honorable cause to found the "NEW CAMEROON". Cameroonians should all join hands irrespective of religion, ethnicity, tribe, region, and other special interests, and then march forward and dismantle this system once and for all, so that we can all begin the arduous task of building the country that our forefathers fought and died for, and voted for in the struggle for independence and reunification. We have an opportunity to build the Ideal Cameroon that filled the dreams of Martin Paul Samba, Rudolf Manga Bell, Ruben Um Nyobè, Felix-Roland Moumié, Osende Afana, Albert Kingué, Ernest Ouandié, EML Endeley, John Ngu Foncha, Ndeh Ntumazah, etc. This would be an inclusive nation that would be the light of Africa, instead of the black sheep that Cameroon under Paul Biya and the anachronistic French-imposed system, is today.

Wednesday, November 30, 2016   *Janvier Tchouteu*

CHAPTER TEN

Addressing "Anglophone Cameroon's" Grievances and the Founding of "The New Cameroon"

The disillusionment, frustration and anger of the peoples West of the River Mungo (former British Southern Cameroonians, former West Cameroonians)—native-born and or indigenous (aboriginal) over the bad treatment they have been receiving in the hands of the usurper system (establishment), a system that is not a reflection of the post-independence government their forefathers had in mind when they voted for independence through (re)unification with former French Cameroun (that became La Republique du Cameroun—the Republic of Cameroun on January 01, 1960) is real, should not be taken lightly and should be addressed in a serious manner. The Biya regime, like its predecessor the Ahidjo regime, and the French-imposed system as a whole, loses any sense of relevance for their gross mismanagement of the reunification and independence project, that half a million Cameroonian civic-nationalists(union-nationalists) and their supporters died fighting for against French colonialism and neocolonialism and the political establishment France set up in Cameroon for its puppets who never fought for, never campaigned for, and never supported the reunification and independence of the lands of the former German Kamerun (British Cameroons and

French Cameroun). So, it is not surprising that the usurper Biya regime, which is the second phase of the oppressive and suppressive system France put in place the country to secure its irrational interests its mafia elites pursue with impunity, is bent on subjugating the last patriotic and civic-nationalists force that made Cameroon's reunification possible (The people of the former Southern Cameroons).

Every opportunity to mitigate or resolve the grievances of Anglophone Cameroonians West of the River Mungo should be seized, even though Cameroonian civic-nationalists (union nationalists who honor our forefathers who fought and died for and who voted for the reunification and independence of the lands of the former German Kamerun), believe that an optimal resolution of the Anglophone problem would be realized under a New Cameroon where the anachronistic French-imposed system has been totally and completely dismantled and where the original objectives of reunification and independence would be the cornerstone of building a Cameroon that is progressive, liberal, free, democratic, just and prosperous.

However, even as we set our sights on these optimal or partial solutions, even as we denounce the French-imposed establishment made up of French-puppets and their collaborators drawn from every region, from every ethnic group, from every religion, and from every linguistic entity in the land; even as we oppose this establishment led and dominated in Cameroon by French-favored groups, we should always bear in mind the fact that the establishment is rejected by the vast majority in all the regions, all the ethnic groups, all the religions and all the linguistic entities in the land. That way, the fight to restore the full rights of the people of former West Cameroon does not become a fight between Anglophones and Francophones; that way, a rejection of the system does not mean Cameroonians hold the Beti-Fang peoples or the Fulani peoples responsible for the Biya and Ahidjo regimes; that way, the grievances of Cameroonians against France's underhanded control of Cameroon does not become translated into a perception of France as an enemy, but rather as a country with the potential of becoming Cameroon's best friend if it makes amends as a moral nation that got led by governments of bad faith that made it fail to become a genuine partner, a France that only needs to turn things around and reconcile with a people whose open heart can even accommodate France as a "Brotherly Nation".

Such a prospect of founding this "New Cameroon" would require honesty, genuineness, and adherence to historical truths from all the parties. The French puppets in Cameroon would have to stop parlaying the distorted history of Cameroon that the anti-Cameroonian forces in the governments of France dished out for them to serve to the Cameroonian people, anti-people narratives that succeeded in brainwashing so many over the decades, lies that denigrated the noble and honorable sacrifices Cameroonian civic-nationalists made for the land's reunification and independence. And even the Anglophobes and Francophobes, and even the Anglophone nationalists and Francophone nationalists (minorities on both sides of the River Mungo) who do not cherish the original goals of reunification and independence would need to cease trying to make enemies out of Anglophone Cameroonians and Francophone Cameroonians.

It does not help when we make comparisons of Cameroon, whose situation is unique in the world, with other countries. Cameroon still has the potential to become the pride of Africa or the curse of the continent. The New Cameroon would become the model around which the future "New Africa would be built. Cameroon stands to become "The Light of Africa". We should not allow the detractors to take our eyes away from the source of that light—Cameroonian Union-Nationalism, whose extension is

African civic-nationalism, the nucleus of the future African economic Union and political confederacy.

Sunday, November 27, 2016   *Janvier Tchouteu*

CHAPTER ELEVEN

The Case for an Independent former British Southern Cameroons Compared to Others

As indicated before, Cameroon's case is unique...In the case of Quebec and Eritrea, they were incorporated into British Canada and Ethiopia as "trophies of war", hence they could or can politely get out (through a plebiscite or referendum)—Quebec; or fight their way out—Eritrea. Eritrea did just that. Britain simply brought South Sudan and Sudan together, two entities that had no history before as a single entity; and it had to take decades of war and millions of deaths for the international community to allow a referendum that allowed South Sudan to go its separate way. And of course, Zanzibar was a British protectorate (a protectorate which in modern international law, is a dependent territory that has been granted local autonomy and some independence while still retaining the sovereignty of a greater sovereign state. The United Kingdom never granted independence to Zanzibar because it never had sovereignty over Zanzibar. the UK simply ended the Protectorate and made provision for full self-government in Zanzibar as an independent country within the Commonwealth. It was the revolutionary government that came to power a month after Zanzibar's independence by overthrowing the pro-British monarch that negotiated a union with Tanganyika, forming a new country called Tanzania. So, Zanzibar could have stayed independent if it wanted to. Southern Cameroons never had that option.

The case in Africa comparable to British Southern Cameroons's is former British Somaliland. Somalis, who had never been united before found their homeland even more divided into three Somali colonial territories (French Somaliland, Italian Somaliland, and British Somaliland.) during the partition of Africa, and the rest as a part of Kenya (North-east Kenya) and Ethiopia (Ogaden). Italian Somaliland became a British Trust Territory, like British Cameroons (British Northern Cameroons and British Southern Cameroons) after World War 2, which Britain administered separately from its protectorate British Somaliland. The Legislative Council of British Somaliland passed a resolution in April 1960 requesting independence and union with the Trust Territory of Somaliland (the former Italian Somaliland), which was scheduled to gain independence on 1 July that 1960. The leaders of British Somaliland and the former Italian Somaliland met and agreed to form a unitary state. However, Britain ended its control over British Somaliland five days before the scheduled unification date, so that the territory was briefly independent as the State of Somaliland before uniting on July 01, 1960, with the Trust Territory of Somaliland (the former Italian Somaliland) to form the Somali Republic (Somalia).

Curiously enough, following the descent of Somalia into a failed state following the exit from power of President Siad Barre, the civil war and the breakdown of the central government, a geopolitical entity emerged in May 1991, calling itself the "Republic of Somaliland", and regarding itself as the successor to former British Somaliland as well as to the State of Somaliland (the short-lived independent state of five days). Yet no country or international organization recognizes it until today. And there are tons of other nominally independent states that are still unrecognized today, but that sacrificed blood to secede from the dominant state they were a part of—Nagorny Karabakh, Transnistria, Donetsk People's Republic, Lugansk People's Republic, and until 2008 Abkhazia and South Ossetia (That Russia and a few countries recognized following the Russo-Georgian war) and Kosovo (recognized by many Western countries), but not by up to half of the world.

In a nutshell, the retarding establishment can only address the grievances of Cameroonians West of the Mungo piecemeal. But a true, fundamental, genuine and overall resolution of Cameroon's No 1, minority problem is possible only in a New Cameroon, a New Cameroon that is possible after all the peoples of Cameroon, irrespective of religion, region, ethnicity or linguistic affiliation join hands and with all seriousness dismantle this French-imposed system that has kept all Cameroonians in a cesspool for close to six decades.

And truth be told, I think the Northwest region is the least conscious of that reality as its politicians confuse the population into continuing the embrace of conflicting forces that divides the ranks of exponents of change there, making them strike blindly most of the time so that the formidable energy that the region generates gets scattered instead of being fully galvanized and channeled to effect cooperation with other forces of change in Cameroon and in building the broader energy that can sweep this monstrous system out of power and realize the New Cameroon. We need to be critical and self-critical; we need to listen to the points of view of others, be open-minded, start calling a spade a spade and turn our backs away even from our family members and tribesmen who are helping to sustain the system in a symbiosis that is leading Cameroon to the abyss. "Long Sense" is not the way forward. It is anachronistic in the cause to found the "New Cameroon" because it smacks of deception and dishonesty that a rational mind finds intolerable.

Monday, November 28, 2016   *Janvier Tchouteu*

CONCLUSION

Nowhere is the hope for the "NEW CAMEROON" glaringly manifested than in the country's National Football Team, which despite the constraints from the French-imposed system (poor infrastructure over the years, poor and corrupt management, etc.), the National Football (National Soccer) Team has made Cameroon an exemplary and perhaps No 1 nation in Africa and one of the best in the world. The players never corrupted their compatriots but gave in their best despite the odds stacked against them. They show the world that Cameroon has the potential to become Africa's light and not the black sheep that the political mafia France set up in the country called the political establishment has made the country to be perceived as for close to six decades.

Cameroon's Anglophone problem or better put, the plight of the two Anglophone provinces of the Northwest and the Southwest, the area that was formerly British Southern Cameroons, highlights the depravity of the system more than any other problem in the country. Yet, strangely enough, the forces that want to tear Cameroon apart and the forces that are running it down while appearing to oppose each other, help to make each other relevant. But the good thing is that these forces are a minority in every part of the country.

The forces that want to tear Cameroon apart are most visible in the English-speaking (Anglophone) part of the country. This force happens to be mostly those who voted against the reunification of British Southern Cameroons and *La Republique du Cameroun*--- The Republic of Cameroun (former French Cameroon) in 1961, and their descendants today. Their agenda to create an independent Southern Cameroons or Ambazonia is not accepted in Anglophone Cameroon (the former British Southern Cameroons, former West Cameroon or the Northwest and Southwest regions today) by those who voted for reunification, most of whom are Cameroonian civic-nationalists, otherwise called union-nationalists or Kamerunists. Most of the Anglophone Kamerunists would like to see a return to the 1961 two-state federation of West Cameroon (English-speaking) and East Cameroon (French Speaking) or a federation of ten or more regions or states, just like most of the Francophone Kamerunists.

Unfortunately, the minority Southern Cameroon irredentists on the one hand and the minority usurper Cameroonian establishment set up by the French political mafia (FrancAfrique) on the other hand, are making each other relevant in their agendas as the anti-Cameroonian Biya regime cloaks the patriotic garment that it has stolen from Cameroon's historic union-nationalists and poses as the force that is trying to keep Cameroon together from the Southern Cameroon secessionists, while the Southern Cameroon irredentists undermine the Cameroonian union-nationalists on both sides of the River Wouri by posing as the force that is going to liberate Anglophone Cameroonians from "Francophones and their regime". Only by Cameroonian union-nationalists exposing and squashing the actions and agendas of both the usurper establishment and the Anglophone irredentists would the "New Cameroon" be born.

GLOSSARY ON CAMEROON

Adamawa

The southernmost province that was carved out of the former Grand North Province. It is a plateau region.

Akonolinga

A town in the Center Province. It is also the capital of the Nyong and Nfomou Division.

Akum

A Ngemba settlement 9 miles from Bamenda along the Bafoussam-Bamenda road. It is also a traditional Ngemba kingdom and the dialect of the people there.

Ambam

A town in the South Province. It is a sub-divisional capital in Ntem Division.

Ashia

Word used by both English and French-speaking Cameroonians to express sympathy, condolence, consolation, encouragement, compassion, harmony, understanding, agreement, thankfulness, and caution.

Bafang   The capital of Upper Nkam Division and a Bamileké kingdom in the West Province.

Bafaw   The principal ethnic group in the area that comprises the Kumba municipality. It is part of the larger Bantu group.

Bafedja   A settlement and Bamileké kingdom in the Nde or Banganté Division, West Province.

Bafoussam   The capital of the West Province and Mifi Division. Also, a traditional Bamileké kingdom.

Bafut   A settlement and traditional Ngemba kingdom about 18 miles from Bamenda in the Northwest Province.

Bakweri   The principal ethnic group in the Fako Division, which is located in the Southwest Province. The Bakwerians are Bantu speaking of the Sawabantu subgroup.

Balengou   Bamileké settlement and kingdom in the

Nde Division, West Province.

Bali
A Chamba settlement and kingdom about 18 miles north of Bamenda, in the Northwest Province.

Bamena
Bamileké settlement and kingdom in the Nde Division, West Province.

Bambili
A settlement and Ngemba kingdom about 9 miles north of Bamenda in the Northwest Province.

Bambui
A Ngemba settlement and kingdom about 6 miles north of Bamenda in the Northwest Province.

Bamenda
The capital of the Northwest Province and Mezam Division.

Bamendjou
Bamileké settlement and kingdom in the Mifi Division, West Province.

Bami (Bamileké)
Diminutive of Bamileké.

Bamileké (Bami)
The most populous semi-Bantu ethnicity and the principal ethnic group in Cameroon. It is also their mother tongue.

Bamilekéland
The western half of the West Province, with fringes in the Northwest and Southwest Provinces. It comprises five

administrative divisions, about ninety traditional kingdoms, and eleven dialectical groupings.

Bamoun   A semi-Bantu ethnicity and one of the principal ethnic groups in Cameroon. Also, their mother tongue.

Bamounland   The Eastern half of the Western province.

Bandekop   A Bamileké settlement and kingdom in Mifi Division, West Province.

Banganté   The largest Bamileké kingdom, the capital of Nde Division, its former name. Found in the West Province.

Bangou   A Bamileké settlement and kingdom in the Upper Nkam Division, West Province.

Bangoua   Bamileké settlement and kingdom in Nde Division, West Province.

Bangoulap   Bamileké settlement and kingdom in Nde Division, West Province.

Bantu   A Large group of Negroid peoples of Central, South, and East Africa that inhabits the forests of the Southwest, Littoral, Center, South, and East

Provinces of Cameroon. Also, the largest constituent of the Negroid or Black race.

Bassa

The principal ethnic group in the Littoral Province. It is Bantu speaking. Also found in the Center Province of Cameroon.

Batoufam

Bamileké kingdom in the Mifi Division, West Province.

Bawok (Bahouok, Bahouoc)

Bamileké kingdoms speaking the Medumba dialects, found in the West and Northwest Provinces. The principal ones are:

- Bawok-Banganté or Banganté-Bawok is a traditional Bamileké kingdom found in the Banganté subdivision, Nde Division. Much of the kingdom is located in the city of Banganté. Following a series of strives in the early twentieth century, it lost most of its territory to the surrounding Bamileké kingdoms, with its subjects migrating to other areas in Cameroon and even founding new kingdoms.

- Bawok-Bali or Bali-Bawok: An

offshoot of the mother kingdom of Bawok-Banganté, founded in 1907 with the help of the friendly Bali-Nyonga kingdom. It is an enclave in the Bali kingdom or *fondom*.

Bayangam   Bamileké settlement and kingdom in the Mifi Division, West Province.

Bazou   Bamileké kingdom in Nde Division, West Province.

Beti   Diminutive of Beti-Pahuin. It is also a subdivision of the Beti-Pahuin group of languages and is broken down further into Ewondo, Eton, Bane, Mbida-Mbane and Mvog-Nyenge.

Beti-Pahuin   Diminuted or shortened to Beti, this group of related peoples constitutes the third principal ethnic group in Cameroon. The ethnic homeland of the Beti-Pahuin people is in the Center and South Provinces, with fringes and enclaves in the East Province. They are Bantu-speaking and comprise the following:
- Beti (Ewondo, Bane, Mbida-Mbane, Mvog-Nyenge, and Eton),
- Fang (Fang proper, Ntumu,

Mvae, and Okak)
- Bulu (Bulu, Fong, Mvele, Zaman, Yebekanga, Yengono, Yembama, Yelinda, Yesum, and Yekebolo.)
- Smaller tribes or ethnic groups Pahuinised by the Beti-Pahuins such as the Baka, Bamvele, Manguissa, Yekaba, Evuzok, Batchanga (Tsinga), Omvang, Yetude peoples.

Beti-Pahuin people are also indigenous in Equatorial Guinea, Gabon and The Republic of Congo.

Betiland   The Beti-Pahuin speaking regions of Cameroon (stretches from the southern half of the Center Province, to the central and eastern parts of the South Province and extend as fringes into the Eastern province), Equatorial Guinea (Rio Muni), Gabon (the northern half), The Republic of Congo (the northwest), and São Tomé and Príncipe.

Biafra   The short-lived Ibo-dominated state that seceded from Nigeria during the 1966–1970 Nigerian Civil War.

Bota   A suburb of Limbe, Fako Division, Southwest Province.

British Cameroons	The western third of the former German Kamerun that fell under British control following the partition of the German colony. It comprised British Northern Cameroons and British Southern Cameroons.
Boumnyebel	A Bassa village in Nyong and Kelle Division, Center Province.
British Northern Cameroons	The Northern half of British Cameroons that voted to unite with Nigeria in 1961, following the controversial United Nations plebiscite in the territory.
British Southern Cameroons	The Southern half of British Cameroons. Became part of the Cameroon Federation in 1961 following a plebiscite that resulted in its reunification with former French Cameroun. It comprises the Northwest and Southwest Provinces of Cameroon.
Buea	The capital town of the Southwest Province and former capital of German Kamerun.
Bulu	One of the peoples of the Beti-Fang ethnic group with a homeland in the South Province.

Cameroonian Pidgin	Also called Cameroonian Creole or Kamtok, it is the Pidgin English spoken in Cameron. It has five variants.
CENER	(*Center National des Etudes et de Recherché*)—Acronym of Cameroon's secret intelligence service (National Center for Studies and Research)—that was changed in 1984 to *Direction Générale de la Recherché Extérieures* (DGRE)—General Directorate for External Research.
Center Province	Central province of Cameroon. Comprises eight divisions.
CNU (Cameroon National Union)	Party formed in 1966 from the merger of the political parties operating in Cameroon. It was headed by the first Cameroonian president Ahmadou Ahidjo.
CPDM (Cameroon People's Democratic Movement)	The CNU renamed in 1985.
CU (Cameroon Union)	Party formed by Ahmadou Ahidjo.
Douala	The largest city, economic capital and capital of Wouri division and Littoral Province.

Duala   A Bantu-speaking people of the
                     Sawabantu subgroup, they are the
                     principal ethnic group of the Wouri
                     Division and the Douala area.

East Cameroon   The French-speaking federal unit of
                     Cameroon from 1961–72. It was formed
                     from former French Cameroun.

East Province   The Southeastern half of Cameroon. The
                     East Province has four divisions with
                     Bertoua as its capital.

Eton   One of the peoples of the Beti-Fang
                     ethnic group. Found in the Center
                     Province.

Ewondo   One of the peoples of the Beti-Fang
                     group. Found in the Center Province of
                     Cameroon.

Extreme North   A province in the far North of
                     Cameroon. It comprises six divisions.

Free French Forces   These were French and Francophone
                     fighters who continued fighting the axis
                     powers of Germany, Italy, and Japan,
                     even after France surrendered and
                     signed an armistice agreement with Nazi
                     Germany in June 1940. It was formed by
                     General Charles De Gaulle, who was a

member of the French cabinet on an official visit to Britain at the time of the surrender. General Charles De Gaulle strongly opposed French capitulation and the armistice signed by the new regime led by Marshall Petain that created the Vichy regime in the South of France, thereby allowing the North of the country to be under German occupation. He urged resistance against German control of France and its collaborationist Vichy puppets. The movement drew recruits mostly from the French empire, especially from French Central Africa, of which French Cameroun was the base at the time, under the new governorship of Jacques Philippe LeClerc. Philippe LeClerc led the Free French Forces' first major victory in the war with the capture in 1941 of Kufra, a town in the then Italian colony of Libya. It incorporated forces of the former Vichy regime in the colonies from 1943 and saw its ranks swollen by Frenchmen after the D-Day landing. The Free French Forces achieved their greatest glory with the liberation of Paris in August 1944, led by the French 2nd Armored Division because it had the least number of blacks in its ranks. By the end of the war, The Free French Movement constituted the fourth largest military force in Europe, fighting against the Axis powers. The right-wing political parties in France have been dominated by its members and the ideology of its founder called Gaullism.

Fulfulde (Fula, Pulaar, Pular, Peul)	A Sene-Gambian language spoken by the Fulani people.
Fulani (Fulani, Fula, Fellata or Peul)	A mixed Negro-Tuareg people inhabiting the Savannah from Sudan to Sene-Gambia, they comprise three groups namely:

The Mbororo, Bororo, Burure or Abore, who are pastoralists.

The Fulanin Gida, Ndoowi'en or Magida, who are fully sedentary communities.

The semi-sedentary Peul people who are agriculturalist and ultimately resume pastoralism, but often form permanent communities.

Foulanis, Fulanis or Peuls are the second most populous ethnic group in Cameroon. Found mostly in the northern provinces of Adamawa, North and Extreme North. Their language is the lingua franca of this part of Cameroon.

Foumbam	The capital of the Noun Division and the Bamounland. Found in the West Province.
Foumbot	Agricultural settlement in the Noun Division.
French Cameroun	The Eastern two-third of the former German Kamerun that fell under the control of the French following the partition of the German colony by Britain and France. It became a French mandatory territory and later trust territory from 1918–1960.
Garoua	The capital of the North Province and Benue Division.
Graffi	Pidgin German word for a grass field. A name often applied collectively to the semi-Bantu peoples of the Northwest and West Provinces of Cameroon.
Graffiland	Cameroonian word for Western High Plateau, Western Highlands, or Bamenda Grassfields. Mountainous grassland region of the Northwest and West Provinces of Cameroon. It comprises the Bamilékéland and Bamounland in the south, and the Ngembaland, Chambaland, and

Tikarland in the north.

Ibo	One of the four principal ethnic groups of Nigeria. Found in the southeast.
Idenau	A town in Fako Division, Southwest Province.
Kamveu	The local council of notables among the different Bamileké kingdoms.
Koufra (Kufra)	An important but isolated Oasis settlement in the southeastern Libyan desert that was of strategic importance for the North African campaign during the Second World War. Its capture from the Italians by the Free French Forces marked the first major battle won by France in the war, thereby boosting General Charles De Gaulle's prestige and the morale of the demoralized anti-Vichy forces.
Koutaba	A settlement in the Bamounland, Noun Division, West Province. Also, a major military and airbase in Cameroon,
Kumba	The largest city in the Southwest Province and capital of Meme Division. It is located about 70 miles north of Limbe.

KNDP (Cameroon National Democratic Party)	Nationalist party in British Cameroons. It led the campaign that realized the reunification of British Southern Cameroons with former French Cameroun.
Limbe	Former Victoria. It is the capital of Fako Division in the Southwest Province.
Littoral	Coastal province of Cameroon. It consists of four divisions.
Loum	An agricultural town in the Mungo Division, in the north of the Littoral Province.
Maguida (Magida)	Name erroneously used for the peoples of the Moslem North that originated from the third group of Fulanis—the Fulanin Gida, comprising the fully sedentary Fulani communities.
Mamfe	The capital of Manyu Division in the Southwest Province.
Manjibo	A Bamoun village in the Noun Division.
Mankon	Mankon is a Ngemba kingdom and part of the city of Bamenda.
Maroua	The capital of the Extreme North Province and Diamare Division.

Mayo Tsanaga	A division in the Extreme North Province of Cameroon.
Mayo Tsava	A division in the Extreme North Province of Cameroon.
Mbengwi	The capital of Momo Division in the Northwest Province.
Mboh	A Bantu-speaking people of the Mungo Division in the Littoral Province, with fringes of their homeland in the Southwest and Western provinces.
Mokolo	Capital of Mayo Tsanaga Division.
Molyko	A suburb of Buea in the Southwest Province.
Mora	The capital of Mayo Tsava Division.
Mutengene	A junction town to Limbe, Buea, and Tiko, in Fako Division, Southwest Province.
Nde	Formerly called Banganté Division. It is found in the West Province of Cameroon.
Ngaoundéré	Capital of the Vina Division and Adamawa Province.

Ngemba	The second most populous peoples of the semi-Bantu group. The Ngemba peoples are found in the northern half of the Cameroon Grassland (Western Highlands), mostly in the Mezam and Momo Divisions of the Northwest Province. The Ngemba people speak closely related dialects.
Ngembaland	The southwestern part of the Northwest Province that is composed of several traditional kingdoms or fondoms speaking closely related dialects.
Nkongsamba	The capital of the Mungo Division of Cameroon. It is also the largest city in the area.
Nkwen	A traditional Ngemba kingdom and part of the city of Bamenda.
North Province	Central of the Grand North Provinces. It comprises four divisions.
Northwest Province	A province from the former Federal unit of West Cameroon and the former territory of British Southern Cameroons. Peopled by semi-Bantu groups of Tikar, Ngemba and Chamba speakers. Their compatriots in the Southwest Province collectively call them 'Graffis'.

Nzui-Mantor	Banganté-Bamileké word for the panther or leopard.
OK (One Cameroon)	An offshoot of the UPC after it was also banned in British Cameroons.
Peul	A French term for Fulani borrowed from the Wolof language.
Semi-Bantu	The unique and unrelated peoples in Africa, comprising the Bamileké, Bamoun, Tikar, Ngemba and Chamba peoples.
Sokolo	A suburb in Limbe, Southwest Province.
South Province	Cameroon's southern coastal province. It comprises the three divisions of Ntem, Ocean and Dja and Lobo.
Southwest Province	Southwestern coastal province of Cameroon. It has four divisions. Formerly a part of British Southern Cameroons and the federal unit of West Cameroon.
Tchollíré	The capital of Rey Bouba Division in the North Province.
Tiko	A coastal town in Fako Division in the Southwest Province.

Tonga	Bamileké settlement and kingdom in the Nde Division, West Province.
Tuareg	A Berber-speaking people of the Mazigh group inhabiting the central Sahara from Southern Algeria and Tripolitania in Libya, to the middle Niger and the northern borders of Nigeria. They moved to the interior of the Sahara Desert to escape the Arab invasion of North Africa in the 7th and 8th century.
UPC (Union of the Populations of the Cameroons)	First national and nationalistic party in Cameroon. The historic UPC was formed in 1948. Banned in 1955, it resorted to an armed struggle that continued well into the late 1960s.
Victoria	The former name of Limbe. Was founded in 1857 by missionaries for the settlement of rescued or freed slaves.
West Province	The southern half of the Western Highlands of Cameroon. It is populated by the Bamileké and Bamoun peoples. It is also Cameroon's cultural and agricultural heartland and is remembered for its historic role as the center of the country's nationalism and liberation struggle against the French Army in the land. It comprises the six divisions of Bamboutous, Menoua, Mifi,

Nde, Noun, and Upper Nkam.

Wolowose   Cameroonian word for a whore.

Wum   The capital of Menchum Division in the
                     Northwest Province.

Yaoundé   Cameroon's second largest city and
                     national capital. Also, the capital of the
                     Center Province and Nfoundi Division.

Made in the USA
Las Vegas, NV
27 September 2021